Broken Lines and Rainbows

poems

Broken Lines and Rainbows

poems

Raja Chakraborty

Hawakal
PUBLISHERS
CALCUTTA   NEW DELHI

Hawakal Publishers

33/1/2 K B Sarani, Mall Road, Calcutta 80
70-B/9 Amritpuri, East of Kailash, New Delhi 65

Email info@hawakal.com
Website www.hawakal.com

First edition October, 2020

Copyright © Raja Chakraborty 2020

Cover art: Shutterstock
Cover design: Bitan Chakraborty

All rights reserved. No part of this publication may be reproduced or transmitted (other than for purposes of review/critique) in any form or by any means, electronic or mechanical, including photocopy, recording, or any information storage and retrieval system without prior permission in writing from the publisher or the copyright holder where applicable.

ISBN: 978-81-948077-3-5

Price: 350 INR | USD 12.99

Between the covers
dreams grow to die.

Papers, a silent witness
of a broken pen....

Contents

A Red Dot

I wrote pages of love.
They did not understand my words.
They did not even read the lines.

Instead they made their own poem of hate,
covered it with torn white flowers and
called it the Angel of Peace.

Not far away from the book,
carelessly shot, a dove lay on the hostile
ground, quivering for life.

A red dot, indulged,
grew in strength.

A Silent Prayer

Stone by stone,
bound by soil
a mountain grows
to kiss the clouds,
to touch the sky
in reverence.
And bring back
tears for the earth
to cry in a
silent prayer
for the forests,
dead and gone.

A Tea Stall Tale

He chanced upon a love
in a roadside tea stall.
His city-bred eyes arrested
by her open rustic stare,
he smiled a half-spoken hello.
Her face hidden behind unruly curls,
her strong hands moving in tandem
with the kettle and cups,
like a floating symphony
rooted him to the spot, smitten.
He let go two homebound buses
and ordered a third cup,
desperately searching for words.
She watched the bespectacled man
with a flutter in her stomach,
as wolf-stories told by her grandma
clouded her throbbing heart.
She waited for a ray of light
through the clouds.
He waited for a smile in return
and the last bus.
Years later as I sat sipping from
a cup in a roadside tea stall,
an old lady behind the stove rumbled
of a stranger on the last bus,
who could not find the words
and a girl whom
a story stopped from being a story.

AFTERMATH

Dank taste of a jaundiced sky
trickling down my throat,
I scratched the stars loose of their
orbits, clawed into the pale
strawberry flesh of a bewildered moon
and chased frightened meteors
down hushed galaxies that
trembled with fear of annihilation.

A silent earth, witness to the
devastation, counted hours, waiting
to be executed, aftermath of outlived
time that has run its course.

ALONE

Coffee on table, roasted beans, cold.
Splayed hand on the armrest, fallen.
Head lolled to a side, vacant stare, locked.
Did the slightly parted lips
hold a sorry smile, mocking itself?

Stale fragrance in the air, stagnant
hung deep on the soiled edge of
the sofa where not so long ago the
creases were warmed by a known
breath; lonely tears in dog-eyes
sat mourning on a corner rug.

A three-day-old newspaper reported.
By then too damned late, as usual.

AMUSEMENT PARK

Roasted garden
lavender corpses
flies celebrate decay.

The Ferris wheel keeps churning
screams reverberate
in ash colored tents.

A rickety gate,
fancily dressed in cobwebs
swayed in the wind.

Standing outside
a tepid mind wondered
whether to cross the threshold.

APOCALYPSE

Frustration has fingers.
It claws into the wounds
to draw fresh blood
to add a little more
red to the wine that
tastes all the same like
stale clots, stacked with
frozen moments of
want and despair, eating
into the periphery, then the
soul of a clobbered mind
still prey to uneasy
rainbows, falsely imagined.

A brazen sunrise peeps
sheepishly, hoping to see
through the dark amber
black clouds standing guard,
it's another nothing day.

BLACK

Walking along the contours of a broken prism
I picked up shards of shattered colors
amidst the patched lines of my palm.
Hues of different shades, shaking with fear
sought refuge in my battered skin
ostensibly fading with each new howl
of ever extending cracks
trying to find comfort in brotherhood.
Their tears ran like mad streams
down my trembling fingers,
forming confused puddles, a palette of
unrecognizable pigments.
It slowly dawned on me that the tone of
raw, unblemished fear is always black.
Ask the shaken rainbow
lost in the smudge of jealous clouds.

CHILDREN OF DESTINY

She was a child of mistake
or so thought the bodies
that made her
and dumped with leftovers
in a roadside bin.
But as luck would have it
or destiny,
she survived the cold night
and thirty years
to be a mother of her own
little children.

No mistakes, she murmured,
as she looked at their
innocent smile
and cried a solitary tear
for two unknown
forever forgotten faces.

CLAUSTROPHOBIC

Walls crash.
Brick and mortars
in my face
strangle light.
Space shrinks
into a funnel,
encroach my fingers
and turn them
into stones.
Flared nostrils
suck on emptiness.
Desperate eyes
looking for a
door somewhere,
I try to push the
dark corners away.
Will the sun ever
rise again in
an open blue sky?

COCAINE

Haze—
it's all about that haze.
A deluge of smoke.
Thick blankets on drowsy eyes.
Weak fingers fondling
misty covers with love and care
in maternal empathy.
World of lies become reality
where pain is shushed
with programmed dreams.
Speaking of dreams, the mind
works in unending circles of
subjugation, taking you deeper
down the dungeon depths until
all you care about is the last puff
gloried into a fatal stupor
only death is scared of.
The haze broadens, adding
one more victory to its pompous flesh
bursting at the seams as
smoke belches out in agony.

Cold stone eulogize a life
that nobody actually lived.
Dead weekly flowers murmur in
agreement with a fragrance so lost.

EVERYDAY GODS

Lopsided, a smile caressed
the corner of her lips
creating a beautiful tangent
bordering on surreal.

My fingers shook
on the canvas.

I have not drawn
a god before.

Here she was, right here.
Her hair ruffled by
the winds, her skin like yours
and mine, mundane.

I could touch her.
Almost.

I would have...

But her eyes
her smoldering eyes

looked right through me
caught my lies.

I was scared.
My brush faltered as it
touched the innocence
of the canvas, pristine
in its emptiness.

She was smiling still—
her lopsided smile
and mocked
all our worships and prayers.

For she knew, art is nothing
but a pretense to hide
our sins, while she dies
everyday in our hands.

FLOWERS IN MY CITY

Steel breathes; so does concrete
in hushed monotones.
Glass reflects, in retrospect.
Fragile balconies shelve potted miseries.
Not all is plastic though.

Amidst the mayhem of motor cars
and multitude of faceless on-goers,
fighting the belching smoke
and putrid air, heavy with broken
promises, behind the ribbed
iron gates, somewhere in a corner
flower always blooms.

Raising its tiny brave head
to greet a grateful sun.

GROW OLD WITH ME

Grow old with me.
Share your wrinkles, greying
hair, your blotched skin.
Take my breath and fill
your empty lungs.
Sing songs we adored,
words fogged into
shabby inheritance.
In the shadow of dimmed
vision let memories play back.
Let the bent fingers meet
in a rickety embrace, touch
to touch; lay your head
on my shrunken shoulders.
I'll carry the load and paint
happy snapshots of lighter times,
just so you forget that we
are dying every day in a slow
waltz, each moment
trespassed in love.

HOLOCAUST

Air at a caustic premium,
gaped mouths sucked at
whatever was left in the
windowless room.
An alien whizz eating up tired minds,
each breath fought the other.
Shocked, bulging eyes, surprised
at the sudden emptiness,
cried fear, flaying, rotten nails
clawing aimlessly at shrunken
chests and souls alike.
Attempts at inhaling drowned
by fits of hollow cough, chaotic
they fell upon one another,
a heap of forsaken humanity
in a tangle of heads, limbs and
torsos, stripped of identity.
Ownership unclaimed, forgotten.
Outside, under a topaz blue sky,
a gentle breeze floated across
careless, happy almost.
Footsteps of another eventual spring,
the trumpets merrily announced.

Middle Class Love

Economy of words always saved me
from exuberance of promises.
She said bring me the universe.
I said it's right here in your eyes.
A noisy childhood taught me
the essence of silence; so when the
sky made swollen faces and the
winds played truant, I simply smiled
and told her to keep the emotions
under tight leash, lest they fly away.
And thus it went through the weather
beaten years. I never promised her the
rainbow and she never got any; funnily
love remained unscathed, evergreen
in every little moment we still share.
The stars kept shining and the moon rose.
We made love in unsaid words.

Notre Dame

Occasional flickers grew in voluptuous
numbers, tongues of naked hunger
hissed and devoured, like a frenzied
pack, rampaging through remnants of
bones and blood alike.

Angry columns of smoke bellowed in
the sky, pillars of fury threatened a
darkness, blacker than dark times.
Crackling notes sang a harsh song
words choking in their own tears.

The wind roared in mirth as the last
vestige of glory crumpled in
hapless disaster, shocked in death.

ODE TO PAIN

Crushed, the wounded flowers
lay bleeding on the ground
waiting for the final sting.

Bees or hyena, who it would be
did not matter, as long as the
cherished hand of relief arrives.

To cleanse the pain with a
swift stroke, quick end is better than
a prolonged epilogue, they know now.

Betrayal is a cruel teacher.
But does it not teach well the worth
of pain!

OF BODY AND MIND

When are you going to grow old?
My body asked me, in protest.
I am tired of use and abuse,
yet you keep going on.

Wings that never rest, scorching the
skies and still ask for more
dragging me along, reckless.

A storm, mid-wind, that does not
know how to stop, a mad river,
hungry for the sea, tearing
shores and roots apart, in search
of an impossible end.

I say, it's the mind, you see
playing games with you and me.

An eternal child who refuses
to grow up and count travelled years
this life has seen and endured.

Of Seasons

Walking back into the spaces
my soul dreams

I saw trees

looking into the skies in search
of light.

Branches holding leaves,

each a story
unfolding into innumerable seasons

that I am.

Of Dreams and Betrayals

I washed my hair in rose water for you.
But you did not come. The man who
came with scissors to chop my locks
was not you.

I put bindi on my forehead and
lavender behind my ears for
you. But you did not come. The
man who came and blotched
the bindi all over my face
was not you.

I draped my first red sari carefully
and waited by the window for
you. But you did not come. The
man who came with brutal hands
to tear it off my innocent body
was not you.

Tell me how many of You are there.
Tell me how many of You will molest
my dreams and not see my tears.
Tell me how many times I have to die
in your hands to find you.

OF GODS AND MEN

I need to die a thousand deaths
to cleanse the sins
and set right the follies, amen.
I need to die a thousand deaths
to be born again
almost perfect but not quite
for it is only thou who
bestowed with perfect imperfections
but never questioned how
ruled ye world ever so perfectly.
Righteous claims gave you the throne
but lest not forget the blood and the bone.
Conspicuous was your chair
devil's forbearer was almost there,
so fought you right to the men
and victory was yours, amen.

Of Mountains and Blue Birds

There was this mountain,
my friend.
Standing tall when I
needed it most.
An umbrella when it rained.
A shadow from the scorching sun.
There for me
every day of my life
to listen in silence to my poems
and embed in its rocks
pages of an ordinary existence
through centuries of
frozen time.
Until the blue birds
found them and
made it their song.

OF MURDER

Green is not a safe number.
Blades of grass can cut you to pieces.
Red, at times, looks ominous on green.
Old rivalries and revenges taken
my grandfather, in his ambitious metaphor
felled a forest to have his no-nonsense,
encumbrance-free hangout, with a dollop
of nature on the fringes, curated!
No one knew the extent of its periphery
his great years included; sad, but true.
So it was all chop, chop, chop and some
more till green was a color in history
and civilization an extinct word
that no dictionary could ever boast of.

Of Trepidations

Low-voltage memory
faltered in its
rusted circuit.

Uncertain fingers
searched the thin air
for hidden routes.

Feeble sparks of
wisdom illuminated a
forgotten corner.

The linen sighed
depressed by the
burden of truth's lies.

OLD AGE HOME BIRTHDAYS

Half a candle
flame, limping
stood shaky on
the plum cake.

Few faded ribbons
pulled out from
the old drawer
lent some color.

Blurred images
looked back
from yellow
photographs.

Someone strumming
'You've a Friend'
faint strains of voices
in the next building.

Drunk in that thought
blowing out the candle
I stood in darkness
and whispered,
happy birthday
to the mirror.

PHOENIX

Thinker of primordial thoughts
basking in the foreknowledge of
disaster, you saw the end as the
beginning of creation, ran full
circle in floating steps and like a
phoenix rose to celebrate again
Bacchus in company, the eternal
soothsayer, warm in embrace
whispering words of unmitigated
wisdom through the tinted glass,
your holy book close to your heart.

POETRY FROM THE OTHER SIDE

They were curious about who I am.
They asked me who I sleep with.
They questioned my integrity
mocked my existence, as if.

But they never wanted to know my
soul and they never saw my poetry.

Instead all they wanted was to break
my lines, castrate them on hypothetical
surgical tables, looking for a befitting label
that suits their carefully arranged
world of words.

A world full of plastic.
They called them emotions.

RAIN

Yellow colored clouds
sadness painted across their
soft cellulite skin
stood outside my window
one grave overcast morning.
Pain in their misty eyes
spoke of untold grief.
They stood like mammoth statues
made of failed promises,
until the winds came
and tore tiny flakes of their flesh
to turn them into
silent tear drops.

I felt on my face
their liquid embrace.
Pleasing touch of an unseen hand
cool as the November rain
washed away my sorrows
with their tears, un-cried still.

RAINBOW

In my monochrome life
rainbow was a
stolen moment with
your memories
between routine chores.
A dead end singing
tunes from good old days
of sunshine and
unplugged laughter
like Roman Holiday
in a corner seat,
fingers talking silently
over shared popcorn
and dreamy eyes
picturing a road
to be travelled together
on a journey unknown.

Some roads never meet.
Some journeys never begin.

RESURRECTION

They had blocked the area
yellow tapes all around.

Guards, sharp eyes, stop lines
the full show.

Butterflies had a tough time
crossing over, I guess even the
air was shy to probe in.

One sparrow, hopping merrily
(as they usually do, you know!),
got pushed away.

Peeved, the sparrow muttered,
"it's only a sapling sprouting"

"Resurrection", the watchdog
solemnly replied.

RETROSPECT

Walking backwards
I saw the street of my childhood.
Grown-ups now, changed.

Skeleton of trees, where we played hide and
seek,
flanked the shrunken shoulders of the street.

Smiling balloons have become
old faces, like a cringed moon
crevices running deep lines of subjugation.

Contours have changed colors.
Dark holes punctured the view where
my friend's house had happily sat.

Where have all the people gone?
The blue skies?

Strange shadows stood like ghosts
and stared with hollow eyes.
No one spoke, silence reigned supreme.
Sounds of sighs filled my ears.

Was someone calling out my name
or is it the winds crying?

Round the bend I found the candy shop,
selling carcasses, the mysterious sweet smell of
lozenges replaced by the pungent
odour of dead dreams.

And the music.
Our street belonged to musicians.
Guitar strings and piano keys, drum beats
at odd hours, a serenade wooing life.
All dead now.

Time, the cruelest player of all
has taken its toll. I walked on, trying to
find my way back, the road is not easy.
But I walk on.

SALVATION

Dark waters have a mind of their own.
As I stand on the bank, I see
my faces floating in them.
They come to me, rest at my feet, talk
fingers touching edges of cold waves.
In silent gestures they tell me how
the water changes color, like faces do.
I look beyond the surface, murky
spasms overrun each other
desperate to hide the lies I told.
Deeper down I see my forgotten wrongs
coralled into black patches, so stubborn
the waves could not erase.
I take off my clothes, my face, my skin
and step into the waves, walk into them
to be one with my true self, purged.

SCARED

When the last bullet crossed
the weeping air and
tore into breathing flesh

they called it an end.

White doves were thrown
against a red sky.
Shells and mortars sang
in harmony.

Peace, scared to be
shot again, stayed in hiding
far from the hollow voices
calling its name.

SONGS OF SILENCE

There was no sound. Even the wind did not breathe.
Leaves tried to form words
but they dissolved in the still
air, like half-born dreams.
Overhead clouds passed by in a silent procession
mourning song-less birds.

Flowers bloomed sans a whisper,
petals woke up in a
complete void. No birth cry was to be heard.
Waves, in the nearby river,
mimicked images from a silent movie,
playing, dancing, chasing each other, as if
in a trance.

Echoes were imagined.
Far away the mountains stood like meditating sages,
lost in silent thoughts.

The boy stared from his window, like every day and
gave the name of a sound to each of them.
His fingers talked and his eyes drew a world where
music played with every step he took.
His lips sang songs that nobody could hear, that
played in his mind alone.

Songs of silence, the skies sang with him
in his soundless world.

STAY AWAKE

Stay awake, the night is yet to come.
In the soft light of a fading sun
see how the waves hug the shore
and bid goodbye with a promise
to meet another time
in some other world,
in some other life.
The hand that touched your heart
the eyes that found poetry in your words
the lips that sang your songs
will come back one day, stay awake
to welcome the moment;
for every departure is a journey
that will find you again on a road
you thought was deserted.

STORY OF THE OTHER ROOM

In another room, same old house
her breath forming stories
of loneliness, she dusted her
memories with care.
Every evening was a moment
in despair, every night
a renewed hope of deliverance.
Her flesh was all she possessed,
her mind a playground of ghosts.
She cried with the yellow light
of the fading ancient bulb
melting into a darkness that
hid her from dying daily
in the crude blaze of an ugly sun
that knows only to shine
in its own futile glory,
oblivious of the dreams it kills
along the perfect symmetry
of its orbit, nonchalant.

STRANGERS

You were right,
I am always
in a crowd, alone.
Faces talk, words travel.
I catch a few
and say the obligatory
hello, hope all good!
Handshakes and
the occasional hug
smelling of brotherhood
posed, may be practiced.
Replies fly back
asking about temperatures
generally, over a
glass of single malt
or coffee, black.
When we part ways
I know the next day
the same face
may just walk by,
my same-said hello
unanswered, not recognized.
I still smile in the evening

shake hands and
say hello, albeit
like the morning
which routinely comes
after every dark night.
Foolish, you say.
That's me, I reply.

THE DREAMER

Rabid smell of rejection
hung heavy in the stagnant air
like a perpetually wet blanket.

Words prepared for love, unused
lay strewn across the road
waiting for the winds to pick up.

Nobody sang the serenade
anymore, music dying young
as the torn strings wept goodbye.

I walked away from the unopened
door, to the comforting corner of my
soul, holding my fallen shadow.

Yet dreams, like a stubborn itch
clung to my foolishness
and refused surrender.

THE FAKIR

On a lonely grey afternoon
I gave away my cycle
to the bully next door.
I gave away my pack of
Hero cards to my
kid brother, unasked.
I started giving away my
possessions, a bag of
marbles, the sling made
of special rubber, kites
stolen from eager hands,
a little bit of smile,
some old tunes my
mother used to sing,
letters I wrote for you
and never posted,
my skin, carefully unwrapped
and my voice, muted.
I gave away till I had
nothing more to give
than my existence.
And naked, last string taken
I moved away leaving
behind a shell
that used to be me.

THE FROG

There was this frog
with large, surprised eyes
that used to come to my doorsteps
now and then
and look in bewilderment
at the immense struggle
we call life, we enact
and at the same instant
catch a fly with one swift movement
of its hidden tongue
and hop back beyond the walls
content with the day's work
satisfaction written smug
on its moist lips.

Sometimes, I wish
I were the frog.

THE GAME

A tired evening slowly descended
camouflaging the scars and wounds
earned through the day, in a
violet haze of treacherous dreams.
Traces of joy, nipped in the bud,
lingered in the acid air, floating
aimlessly. Random windows threw
shades of yellow on the dark street
pushing against the gloom of the night
trying to get foothold.
A voice somewhere, in dull monotony,
mimicked a lullaby that mothers sang.
Shadows spoke in whispers.
Uncertain words. Dead eyes watched
from a distance and stored in memory
every little detail of the next prey.
The steely silence was broken by a
scampering mouse, the hungry cat hot
on its tail. The game was on.

JOKER

Don't play your hands! Hold them back. The next turn may throw a tangent at you—an ellipse perhaps or a hexagon—all clever traps, embroidered in fancy names. Be warned. Stay calm, let your face be a mask—your eyes roving watchtowers—looking out for now pristine waves to show their ugly heads—frothing at the mouth, and then you strike with the finesse of a wizard. A lethal flurry of delicate fingers—a blur slowed down to perfection—brutally sweet like a crescendo reaching its glory. Lay bare your hand, your masterpiece, for, in the end, the joker takes it all.

THE KILL

Have you seen the eagle soar
scaling the brazen sky with infinite ease.
Its powerful wings conquering gales
and ferocious winds in majestic harmony,
a spot in the blue horizon, gliding like
a trained dancer, specter of gods, a
guided meteor, how it swoops down, a
stroke of lightning, earth-bound, a spear
unfurled, to take its prey in one sudden
sweep and vanish in the wild abandon.

Moments of beautiful madness
or sanity, will be judged in perspective,
but to an untrained eye a lifetime in a flash
that stays lifelong to haunt.

THE LAST SONG

And he sang, standing barefoot, on the edge of the cliff. He sang to the skies, to the darkness beneath, his voice echoing of ragged mountain walls, caressing fog-wrapped valleys. He sang full-throated, chest heaving up and down like bellows pumping in maddening harmony. Chords straining against swirling winds, riding them, spreading out far and wide, a floating cascade of intricate patterns woven by his soul.

He sang to the stars and the moon and the meadows, piano ribs tickling long-dead memories. He sang, head tilted back, eyes closed, arms open and stretched out as if to take the universe in its fold.He sang of broken hearts and broken dreams. He sang of battles and bonhomie—of promises and betrayals—of glories and grey wounds.

He sang for the long lost soul. He sang for love. He sang for you and me. He sang for himself.

His voice a melodious magnificence, gentle yet strong, overflowing undercurrent of frozen passions, weaved a magic spell, profound in its levity. A single tear welled up, poised for a dew-drop moment, crept down his hollow cheek, to the ground where his feet rested, a velvet mosaic, finding its way through the grass, flowing down to meet the river below.

A journey on an oh-so traversed path, littered with fallen leaves, fallen in the quest to meet eternity.

The Maze

When ghosts from the past
come calling, I smell
wild flowers in a blue haze.
I talk to them about lost
shadows, they tell me of
broken pieces of puzzle
they found, scattered
pictures form and dissolve
in my head, vapours.
The canvas keeps changing.
I draw a river which I never
crossed, yet my feet are damp.
I see a house with no walls
an empty chair sits dead-center
rocking silently, counting
forgotten heartbeats.
Voices whisper shapeless vowels.
There's a shriek somewhere
calling again and again.
Relentless, stubborn, sharp
etching deep wounds with
expert brush strokes.
Did you know scars make roads
for me to take
one step at a time into the maze
where all will be lost one day.

THE PSHYCHO

Like a raging bull anger roared
in his chest,
his face a placid ocean.

Cold eyes, storm-crazed
mapped a turbulent mind
straining at the leash, hungry.

Tick-tock of the grandfather
clock hammering inside his head
he counted the tensed seconds.

A smile, beautifully cruel, licked
the corner of his thin lips, the vile
tongue moistened its borders
a viper ready to strike.

As blood filled the gutter
his child-face, tauntingly innocent
did not believe the hands.

Absent-minded he swayed to
the tune of howling winds
dreaming of a nightmare.

THE RAIN SONG

A floodgate opened.
Debris from the past
pushed time twenty years
back into a youth
where love happily tweeted
on unlikely branches
and the sky never
faded into oblivion.
One unreasonable summer
hot like hell fire
all the trees died.
A bird lost its home
and belongings; sad it
carried its song to the
river for the waves to
take it to unseen shores.
Twenty monsoons later
the ocean returned
the song, moss-covered.
On a forlorn beach
a lone seagull picked up
the tune in its wings
and flew to the deep blue
of the unending sky
for the clouds to sing
their rain song.

THE STATUE

In the midst of the busting street
people pushing for space in their own
bubble, on the narrow pavement,
heads down, conversing on phones
stuck to ears, like extended
appendages, protruding
cars wheezing by, horns blaring
patterned mayhem ruling roost,
stood the man, silent, stoic, somber
oblivious almost of life.
A statue in flesh and blood
in a strange world of his own
where words were not to be spoken
but heard in the silence of the
mind, his ragged robe holding on
to the last signs of what we call
civilization and watched with eyes
that saw beyond the madness
and looked for an ocean where truth
drowned, inch by inch, in its watery grave.

TREE

Age befools
so does the mind.

Where do I look for sanity?

Ancient waters
tell me your secrets
that your depths have hidden so well.

I searched the mountains
for the first stone

found mud instead, not truth.

Miles traveled are like dreams
that someone saw for you.

I see my footsteps
in an alien sky.

The tree is still there, on every road
standing like a mute surrender

waiting for its shadow
to merge with the ashes.

Perhaps that's what I seek.
Perhaps that's who I am.

THE WATCHERS

A crowd was gathering
furtively poking
in nervous curiosity.
Questions were left hanging
in the uncomfortable air.
Answers came by—
wild guesses and
considered opinions;
abundant advices too!
Mobile clicks were random
pushing hands jostling
for a better position
the crowd like vultures
sensing death and a meal
closed in
careless feet almost touching
the trickle of blood.
A distant ambulance hooting
ferociously passed by.
A momentary distraction
the crowd got back to its job
of watching motionless.
The morning paper reporting

a reckless car and
a missing someone
was digested over
a cup of hot tea.
The school bus was on time
cackle of young voices
matched the birds
caring mothers watchful.
Breakfast taken
lunch boxes in hand
office goers in serious hurry
flashed goodbye smiles
to the waiting eyes at doors.
Another day rolled out.
Everything moved on fine
without missing a beat, as always.

THE WHISKY SONG

As the yellow liquid
tickled the chords
a sonata formed.
Fumes of fancy
scored the outline
of a song.
Fingers dripping
with excitement
strummed airborne
keys, lips flushed
searched a voice.

Hushed silence trembling
in anticipation, edgy
tapped its restless
feet while words
dressed up in laces,
each beautiful as a
sun-kissed morning.

And then like
a spring unfurled
the baritone took over

cascading down
in torrents of
honey-soaked notes
that the heart sang
oblivious of the sky
and the moon
and the stars
unstoppable in its
naked glory.

THESE ASHES

These ashes that you see
was once a man.

He was the master, power his slave.
His eyes commanded legions.
His voice carried far and wide
drawing hordes to his footsteps.
His shadow bestowed promise of
an unknown heaven.

These ashes that you see
scattered, lost

was once all that we make gods with,
omnipotent in its absolute deliverance.
Heroic deeds and valour his garment
he shone like Apollo
driving away devils and demons
and dark nights barehanded, so the
sun could shine, unobstructed.

These ashes that you see, alas
is nothing but ashes now
waiting for obliteration in
the same nonchalant soil that has
buried the history of gods
and men alike, for ages.

THIS SIDE OF THE DAY

This side of the day
butterflies, wobbly from thirst,
sought pregnant flowers
to dip in and swallow all the
honey that love produced.

This side of the day
the monstrous summer sun,
on a murderous spree, has
sent an army of scorching rays
to shrink all the petals
to utter nothingness.

This side of the day
a defiant breeze unceremoniously
plundered the pollens and
scattered them all across the
desert to die in the sand.

And yet, this side of the day
a new love whispered soft words
and floated them on the
wings of a Red-breast to look
for hope in the blue wilderness.

TOUCHING GROUND

Surrounded by thousand lights
he wrote darkness.
Sitting amidst myriad sounds
he sang silence.

That's how he lived, in stark
opposites and called it his reality
where pictures seldom spoke truth
and eyes did not see in plain vision.

Yet his skies were blue, bluer than mine.
His rivers carried fairy tales and
in moments of deepest despair
hope knocked on his door to say hello.

And he embraced life like a lover
cajoling, flirting, whispering soft words
with death, his ubiquitous bedfellow
holding on strong to him, touching ground.

TRAPPED

I did not know
the color of loneliness
is blue.
Like a deep
dark expanse
it permeates
the skin,
runs through
the veins
till it reaches
the eyes.

And then
the light goes
to leave
behind a trail
where blue
becomes black.

You start living
in your
own shadow
trapped.

UNTOLD

I sat on a park bench
with her shadow playing with god's children.
The wind sashayed in the breeze
rhythmic in its cosmic breathing,
carrying their laughter far and wide.
I looked at the watch, furtively, knowing
time always flies like meandering birds
crossing oceans for shores that
only dreams can dream of.
She suddenly laid down on the
jeweled bed of grass to sing to the
butterflies her favorite lullaby.
A wistful tune spread across the skies
touching tree-tops, clouds, hearts.
I woke up in my slumber, eyes shut
like shells who forgot the pearls.
A gentle wave hushed my muted words
and receded, leaving behind her
memories wrapped in new born flowers.
The bench knows it all, its wrinkles
weaving tales that are never told.

WALK OF LIFE

Roads I walk
turn into mud
cling to my
skin like an
interrupted story
left midway
that years and
the sun has baked
to little morsels
of a picture
somebody forgot
to finish.

When you
find me with
limbs stuck in
an unfinished
movement, know
that what began
in me finishes
with you, like
tress that groom
seeds to prosper
and tell their story.

WASTED

Love
like hushed pregnancy
walked heavy.
Stone-pelters
had a field day
hollering blasphemy.
Two lines of blood
met in a deserted land,
wasted.

Gods cried shaded tears and
called it an eclipse
where light devours itself
in a shame
that even the darkest nights
could not hide.

WHEN YOU SAY NOTHING AT ALL

In deep recesses of soul
thoughts lie in hibernation.

Each cell emote.
Visions shed shells, meaning.

Scriptures are written
in blood and sweat of everyday living.

Mosaics invade heart chambers
in intricate cosmic patterns

and coagulate
stubborn blocks of alphabets.

Somewhere in the forest
words lose way.

Lips die, unused.
Empty pages flutter in silence.

www.ingramcontent.com/pod-product-compliance
Lightning Source LLC
LaVergne TN
LVHW040210180726
843489LV00007B/2801